# OAKHAM

★ ★ ★

# A GUIDE AND HISTORY

★ ★ ★

*by*
T. H. McK. Clough
*Curator of the Rutland County Museum*

Rutland County Council
1999

*Fig. 1. Oakham Castle from the south-east in about 1880, before the magistrates' court had been built, and with the Tudor window in the east wall still in use.*

# OAKHAM CASTLE

## A GUIDE AND HISTORY

"At Oakham there is a certain castle, well walled, and in that castle are a hall, four rooms, a chapel, a kitchen, two stables, a barn for hay, a house for prisoners – the county gaol, a room for the gate-keeper, and a drawbridge with iron chains. The castle contains within its walls an estimated two acres of ground. The same is called the manor of Oakham. Outside the castle is a garden, and fish ponds and a moat."

(AD 1340)

## TOWN AND CASTLE

The Great Hall of Oakham Castle is well known as one of the finest examples of Norman domestic architecture in England. It is all that survives today of an important early medieval fortified manor house, and was built by Walkelin de Ferrers soon after 1180, in the reign of Henry II. The uneven surface of the grass-covered enclosure in the midst of which it now stands shows that the castle buildings were once very much more extensive. Contemporary records, such as the details survey in an inquisition or enquiry of 1340, from which the extract above has been taken, confirm this. Archaeological excavation, although limited in scale, has provided material evidence of some of these buildings. In other cases the documents tell of their construction or repair, particularly when, as happened from time to time, the castle and manor of Oakham were in the hands of the king.

This history brings together some of this evidence to illustrate the rise and fall of Oakham Castle as the administrative, legal and manorial centre of Rutland, and pieces together the sequence of those who held it as lords of the manor over a period of a thousand years.

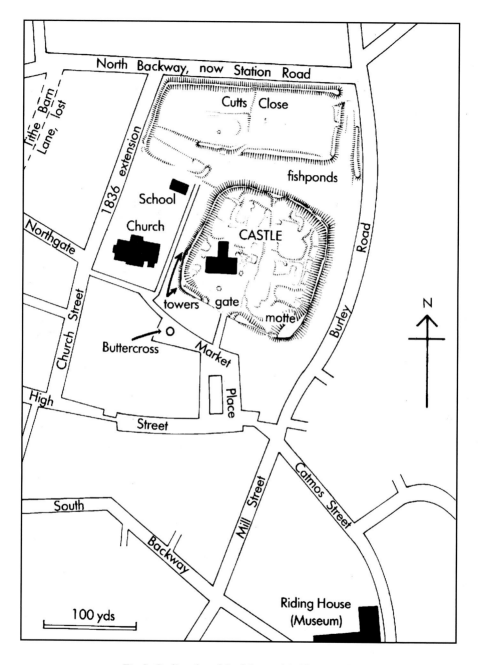

*Fig. 2. Outline plan of the defences of Oakham Castle in relation to the town in the nineteenth century.*

Oakham Castle stands in a central position in this small market town, the county town of Rutland. Nowadays it is somewhat sheltered from the business of modern traffic and commerce, but once it was the focus of such activity. For around the castle in medieval times there were houses and workshops, and this, with the market place, was the busiest part of the town. The manor included farmland, woods and enclosed parks stocked with deer; it also possessed a windmill and a watermill. A number of hamlets and farmsteads were occupied by tenants of the lord of the manor, who in turn held Oakham as a tenant of the king.

There is little enough evidence for the detailed history of Oakham in this early period, but we can reconstruct the general sequence of events. The most important factor is that before the Norman conquest in 1066 Oakham formed part of that property in Rutland which had become the dowry of the Anglo-Saxon queens of England. How this came about is obscure, but it was certainly in royal hands by the tenth century. There is some evidence to suggest that it may have been controlled by the kings of Mercia even earlier than this. Rutland was certainly the dowry successively of Aelfthryth, the wife of Edgar (959-75); Emma, the wife first of Aethelred II (whom she married in 1002) and then of Cnut (1016-35); and Edith, the wife of Edward the Confessor (1042-66), from whom the Rutland village of Edith Weston takes its name.

We do not know whether there was any royal settlement at Oakham early in the tenth century. However, the discovery in 1749 of an important hoard of late Saxon silver pennies, now thought to have been deposited in about 980, suggests a degree of prosperity in Oakham at the time. By then we may be sure that the manor was centred at Oakham. Pre-conquest pottery from excavations on the side of the Post Office and elsewhere in the town provides additional evidence for this. The name of the town is of Saxon origin, and appears to mean "Occa's homestead".

The first mention of royal buildings here comes in Domesday Book, compiled for William I in 1086. Here it is recorded that in "Ocheham" the king had two ploughs belonging to the hall. This hall was not the fine stone building which stands today, for that was not built until a century later. It must have been a royal hall, either dating from before the death of Edith in 1075 and possibly of pre-conquest date, or built by William I after he had acquired the property in that year. What it was like we do not know, but it is likely to have been a substantial timber building, on the lines of other halls of the period known from archaeological evidence elsewhere.

At this time the defences probably took the form of a motte and bailey castle. The hall and other domestic buildings will have been within the bailey earthworks. The motte or mound, surmounted by a strong wooden keep or tower and further defended by a ditch, was at one end. Indeed, the earliest identifiable phase of the existing Oakham earthworks consists of the much mutilated motte and ditch of just such a castle in the south-east corner of the present enclosure. Here the remains of the motte still form the highest and thickest part of the walled ramparts into which it was later incorporated. It is now supported on the outside by a high retaining wall, much overgrown, but visible from the south end of the Burley Road car park. On the inside, the line of the ditch which surrounded it is clearly to be seen.

This form of motte and bailey castle is typical of the early medieval period. In Rutland there are others on a smaller scale at Alstoe (between Burley and Cottesmore), and at Castle Hill, near Uppingham, besides a more complex monument close to the church at Essendine. All are now on private land.

Today we approach the castle by a lane from the Market Place, and pass into the inner bailey through a stone gateway of thirteenth century form. It was rebuilt by George Villiers, who bought the manor in 1621, and who later became Duke of Buckingham. The pediment which he placed above it matches two other gateways which he erected at entrances to the park at Burley-on-the-Hill. The wrought iron gates which hang here date from 1872, when the gateway was again rebuilt. It was then that the horseshoes which hitherto had been fixed to the wooden gates and to the castle door, as shown in Buck's engraving of 1730, were moved inside to join the many others hanging on the walls.

Although the modern post office and other buildings in the Market Place obscure the line of the ditch on this, the south side of the castle, we may presume that this gateway corresponds with the site of the drawbridge. There is no other principal entrance to the inner bailey, although there may have been at least one postern door, in the west wall of the defences near the church. A blocked gateway in the south-east corner, of uncertain but not original date, gave access to a farmyard off Burley Road, and was used until the mid twentieth century to graze prize cattle on the lush grass within the bailey. That there had been some grazing available here from the late medieval period onwards is shown by surviving documents, which give assessments of its annual value.

The line of the ditch was confirmed during archaeological work while the post office was being built in 1953-54. The principal find was a fine medieval carved stone head, which it is thought belongs to one of the musicians whose

*Fig. 3. Castle Lane in the early years of this century (photograph by Frith).*

figures decorate the interior of the Great Hall. Other finds included fragmentary medieval pottery, and a selection of leather soles and uppers from shoes of various sizes and types. Early photographs show that both sides of Castle Lane were later lined by stone buildings, as the moat gradually became filled in and houses encroached on the disused defences.

The moat is also lost to the east of the castle, this time beneath a modern car park beside Burley Road. However, the remains of the stone curtain wall, dating from the thirteenth century, can be seen as well here as anywhere. In the absence of archaeological work it remains unknown whether the defences were completely rebuilt or whether the wall was built up against the existing earthworks. Probably most of the bank that slopes up to the wall is composed of stone and rubble that has collapsed from the wall. As it is today, this wall is of more than one period, and different stretches of masonry of varying quality can readily be identified; most are defined by straight or butt joints. One possible explanation for this is that there may have been several external semicircular bastions, perhaps two or three in number, at intervals along this side, which were removed at an unknown date. This would agree with the evidence of the western defences, where the remains of two such towers still survive.

North of the inner bailey, and defended by earthworks which have suffered a certain amount of more recent remodelling, there is a large outer court or bailey, now known as Cutts Close. This is used as a recreation ground, and the town fairs are held here, as also by tradition is the Boxing Day meet of the Cottesmore Hunt. There is little doubt that it was the site of the garden and, in its lower parts where the moat widens, the fishponds referred to in 1340 and in other inquisitions of fourteenth century and later date. Fishponds, sometimes very complex, were a normal adjunct to any large domestic or ecclesiastical establishment. We know from the bones found during archaeological excavations on such sites that the fish bred in them made an important contribution to the tables and the diet of the times. Fishponds are amongst the most common types of medieval earthwork to have survived. Those which served the Bishop of Lincoln's palace at Lyddington are some of the best preserved in Rutland.

On the western side of the castle enclosure stands the original Oakham School building. This, with its sister foundation at Uppingham, was established in 1584 by Robert Johnson, rector of North Luffenham, and later Archdeacon of Leicester. South of the school stands the parish church. Originally, as we shall see below, the church formed part of the manor, and the fact that the outer earthworks of Cutts Close make as if to enclose it may

*Fig. 4. The north-west corner of the castle earthworks, showing the moat, with Oakham church and the original school building (from a collotype plate).*

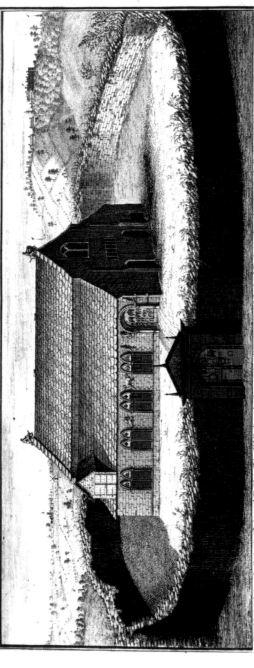

*Fig. 5. S. & N. Buck's engraving of Oakham Castle, 1730, with the doorway in its original position.*

indicate that they were already there by the time that William II alienated the church and its lands from the rest of the manor at the end of the eleventh century.

The most interesting feature of the inner fortifications on the west side is the survival, ignored in most accounts of the castle, of two rounded defensive towers, now overgrown and mutilated. It is the presence of these, one opposite the church and the other at the south-west corner, which suggests that there may have been more such towers along this curtain wall. Most of the trees and growth on the ramparts have sprung up since the late nineteenth century.

A path by the churchyard leads one back through Church Passage to the Market Place, where stand the Buttercross and stocks, and completes this circuit of the castle defences.

*    *    *

## THE GREAT HALL

Most visitors, on passing through the ornamental gates of Oakham Castle for the first time, will remark on two facts. First, the apparent spaciousness of the area which the ramparts enclose; and secondly the absence of any striking stone towers, walls or fortifications such as are generally associated with medieval castles. Oakham was never conceived as a castle in the sense of a highly fortified stronghold. Its character was domestic and residential, with the Great Hall always the centre of social and manorial activity.

The range of buildings which formerly stood around the hall is well described in the account of 1340 already referred to. Some of them, such as the stables, were probably timber buildings, but others, like the hall, will have been of stone.

There was probably an open stone-set courtyard in front of the hall when it was built, which served as a place of assembly, arrival and departure. Looking at the building from the gateway, one would have seen the main doorway where the right-hand window now is, not at the centre of the south wall. The entrance would thus have been at the low end of the hall. When it was moved and why appears not to be recorded; it was at some time between 1730, when Buck's engraving showing it in its original position was published, and 1847 when John Clayton made measured plans and elevations. Similar plans by Henry Dryden were used by the Rev. C. H. Hartshorne in his paper on Oakham Castle published in the *Archaeological Journal* for 1848. Possibly it was an alteration made when new court fittings were put in, and a Grand Jury room added, probably in the early years of the nineteenth century.

Indeed, the walls, both inside and out, provide evidence for many alterations over the centuries. Only at one point on the north wall, at its western end, does any of the original polychrome masonry survive. Here one can see the regular use of warm red ironstone blocks interspersed with single courses of fine pale ashlar work, making the most of the differing colours of the two types of stone. The jumbled and confused masonry of the south wall, on the other hand, preserves hardly anything in an original state.

Two stone finial carvings at the ends of the roof ridge are seen to their best advantage from the south. Together with other carvings now attached to the south wall of the hall, they form part of the repertoire of late twelfth century sculpture at Oakham which is so important for dating the building, and which is described in detail below. Further dating evidence is provided by the two-light windows with their extensive use of dog-tooth ornament. Rarely noticed are the pairs of sensitively modelled heads at the foot of each gable of the nave roof, on its north side, which are very similar in style and treatment to some of the work inside the building.

The greatest surprise for the visitor, on entering the hall, is to find the walls hung with over 200 massive horseshoes, bearing the names and dates of peers of the realm and of royalty who have paid the unique forfeit due to the lord of the manor of Oakham. The origins and history of this ancient custom are discussed, and the horseshoes are listed, in a companion booklet.

The hall is a lofty building divided into nave and aisles by two arcades, each with three massive stone columns. The stone flagged floor of the hall today is in two levels, a feature resulting from a restoration of the castle completed in 1911 under the direction of William Weir of London. The lower level approximates to the original, and enables the moulded bases of the columns to be seen.

The carved figures of six musicians, each playing a different instrument, rest above the capitals of the columns, and the arches rise from elaborate corbels on the end walls. Grotesque faces peer down from unexpected corners as mischievously now as they have for 800 years. The sculpture is described in detail at the end of this guide by Robin Emmerson.

The east wall, which was found to be in a poor state, was extensively repaired in 1911. Twin doorways in this wall, which are now blocked but which once led to a range of kitchen buildings, were also refurbished at the same time. Excavations outside the east end of the hall have produced medieval pottery and small finds, such as part of a pair of bronze nutcrackers or five small bone spoons, dating from the hey-day of the castle in the thirteenth and fourteenth centuries. This archaeological evidence confirms the domestic nature of the buildings.

At the north-east corner of the hall, a stairway must have led to the doorway at first-floor level which can be seen on the inside. A ledge nearby shows where a small gallery or landing once served that doorway, which may have provided access to rooms over the adjoining buildings. The collapse of this corner of the hall at an unknown date and its subsequent rebuilding, for which there is structural evidence, has made it difficult to understand the original arrangement of this end of the hall. It does, however, seem certain that there was never a screens passage or gallery extending the full width of the hall as may be found elsewhere.

At the north-west corner of the hall, beside the judge's bench, a doorway, which is equipped on the far side with an original twelfth century arch comparable to others in the building, led to a solar block providing more private accommodation – perhaps the "four rooms" of 1340, and possibly also the chapel, for the use of the lord and his principal guests. The exterior face of this west gable wall provides further evidence to suggest that this block was of two storeys. Today, this doorway leads to twin cells, dating probably from the early nineteenth century, which still occasionally fulfil that function, and are not open to the public. The corresponding doorway in the south-west corner is apparently of recent origin. It leads to the modern private apartments used by the judge, which were erected on the site of earlier lean-to buildings.

Opposite the present entrance door, another arched doorway, which may or may not be in its original position, leads to the magistrates' courtroom and retiring room. There was already a building, the Grand Jury room, on this site in 1848, described on Dryden's plan as "modern", and probably dating from about 1811. It was rather less than half the size of the present apartments, which were built towards the end of the nineteenth century, but which may include part of the earlier structure. New court fittings were provided here in the mid twentieth century.

The present court fittings at the west end of the Great Hall were designed to accommodate Assizes and Quarter Sessions, with judge's bench, jury benches, witness stand, and dock. They are seldom used for the equivalent business of the Crown Court today, but may be used as a second magistrates' court or for coroner's inquests. For this purpose they are less formidable than the drab brown-stained barricades surmounted by rows of spikes which preceded them, and which are illustrated in late nineteenth century photographs. A further set of court fittings which had occupied the east end of the Great Hall was removed as part of the 1911 restoration.

By the early sixteenth century, the hall probably served hardly any domestic purpose, if we read the documents of the period correctly. Burley-on-the-Hill eventually became the residence of the lord of the manor, and the hall was "convenient to be kept upholden" largely because of the courts which were held here. It was at this time, or perhaps towards the end of the century, that a six-light rectangular window, similar in style to windows found in Rutland houses of this date, was inserted in the east wall to light the hall better. The original two-light window above it was probably blocked up at the same time. The stone mullions of the sixteenth century window can be seen on the outside of the east wall; it remained in use until the beginning of this century, when it was blocked in its turn and the original window reopened. An early photograph shows that when in use it had been protected by board shutters (fig. 1).

Finally, the roof is almost entirely made of recent materials, although one or two of the main beams may survive from the restoration carried out by the Duke of Buckingham after he acquired Oakham in 1621. The early dormer windows in the north and south aisle roofs are possibly early nineteenth century insertions, but like the single dormer shown in Buck's 1730 engraving, they were also formerly protected by wooden shutters. They were re-made in 1911. In 1980, the hall was completely rewired and redecorated, the horseshoes were cleaned, restored where necessary, and rehung, and the opportunity was taken to clean and inspect not only the sculptures but also the timber work. No evidence was found to support a suggestion that there was originally a clerestory above the arcades to provide additional windows, and this possibility is now thought to be unlikely. However, it is clear that the roof did originally fall in two separate pitches as it does now, and we know from documentary sources that it was covered with Collyweston tiles.

★     ★     ★

## THE PAGES OF HISTORY

We can see something of the history and development of Oakham Castle and its Great Hall from the building itself and its surroundings. It is, however, to historical documents from the twelfth century onwards that we must turn to

*Fig. 6. A modern view of the east wall of the castle.*

seek the intimate detail which alone enables us to put life into the past and to put Oakham, and Rutland, into historical perspective.

The castle was the residence of the lord of the manor, but it was also much more. It was the administrative centre first of the manor of Oakham, with its own courts and system of self-government, and also of the emerging county of Rutland. This was one of the last parts of England to be integrated into the shire county system – perhaps not until the later twelfth century, just when Walkelin de Ferrers was lord of the manor and building his castle. It was here also that the officers of royal law and justice held courts, assizes and inquisitions. The first recorded assize in Rutland was held in 1229, and the pleas of the Forest of Rutland were heard here at least as early as 1249.

A gaol was an inescapable necessity, and the royal gaol for Rutland was within the grounds of Oakham Castle. It was not always run in the best interests of justice; we hear, for example, that in 1208-9 the Sheriff of Rutland was in trouble because he was not holding certain prisoners who had been delivered to him by the foresters of the royal forest of Rutland to guard.

Some of the foresters, by all accounts, were undesirable men. One of the leaset savoury was Peter de Neville, Keeper of the Forest, against whom there is a most lengthy series of complaints in the pleas of the forest of 1269. Some of his offences, although not trivial, were of a usual nature, such as making off with the king's deer, and sending his dogs into the manor of Oakham. His father Hasculf had done much the same. Peter, on the other hand, had evidently taken the law of the forest even more into his own hands. He misappropriated the proceeds of fines which were properly due to the king, levied unwarranted fines, and imprisoned offenders in a prison of his own at Allexton in the most miserable conditions. It is specifically complained in 1269 that the castle at Oakham should be the place of detention for all who offended against the forest laws, for example by poaching or trespass.

Such offenders in later years were certainly held in Oakham gaol. Some, among them men of the cloth, were able to secure their release on bail, such as the parson of Knossington in 1320, the parson of Stapleford in 1322, and the master of the Hospital of Burton St. Lazarus (near Melton Mowbray) in 1339.

Bail could be granted even to prisoners held for capital offences. There are many instances recorded in the Close Rolls of men taken for murder, a relatively common offence, being released on bail. On one occasion, in 1269, twelve men were held for the murder of a single victim. Others were able to escape royal justice by different means: in 1290, Nicholas de Weston, held at Oakham and charged with various robberies, larcenies and homicides, purged his innocence before the Bishop of Lincoln in accordance with the privilege of the clergy. Yet others were less fortunate: in 1254, the Sheriff of Northampton was directed to collect William Koc from Oakham gaol and deliver him under a sure guard to Newgate.

The royal eye was never far distant in this period, for the king and his court travelled constantly throughout the land. King John had been at Oakham in 1206, and Henry III, who granted Oakham to his younger brother Richard, Earl of Cornwall, came here at least seven times between 1219 and 1258. When he came in 1244, instructions were sent ahead from Oakham to the Sheriff of Northampton to buy three suitable cups to be ready for the king's arrival there. All the necessary apartments had to be kept in order and supplied with provisions for such occasions – the records note the taking of a tun of wine to Oakham in 1269.

What was more important, and most costly, was the maintenance of the buildings. These were unsettled times, and the authority of the king was far from secure. Oakham, in the hands of Henry III's brother, Richard, was not untouched by the events of the Baron's War in which Simon de Montfort played such a part. In local disturbances in 1264, the hall was damaged by fire. Richard, who died in 1272, may not have lived to see the damage fully repaired, for in 1275 there were complaints that some of the money levied in the hundred of Martinsley (in which Oakham was situated) had been misappropriated.

Richard was succeeded as Earl of Cornwall by his son Edmund, who died in 1300. There was the usual inquisition post mortem, or enquiry following his death, into his lands and property, which the king assigned to his widow in dower. The garden, fishponds, windmill and watermill belonging to the manor, as well as the deer parks, are all mentioned. Later inquisitions and other royal records give us more information of a similar nature. For it is during the troubled years of the fourteenth century that we find more specific references to Oakham Castle than at any other period.

Shortly after the accession of Edward II in 1307, there was a general order to the keepers of castles, Oakham included, to fortify them and guard them safely. Although the curtain wall defences of the inner bailey were probably complete by then, it is possible that some further work was done. There was rebellion in 1321, but by the following year the situation appeared to have eased sufficiently to allow the "munition of men" to be removed from the castles affected. It was, however, still necessary to keep the castle as carefully as before. Stocks of food and other supplies were to be maintained. The keeper

keeper was responsible for selling perishables and buying fresh in their place. No doubt the weekly markets, held every Monday and Saturday, as had been allowed in 1252, saw much of this trade. In 1323, Edward II visited Oakham, safe in the knowledge that an inquisition in the previous year had found no opponents to the king in Rutland.

Perhaps this was no surprise, for Hugh de Audley had just been removed from possession of the manor following a quarrel with the Despensers, the king's advisers. With Oakham in his own hands, the king appointed Ivo de Aldeburgh constable of the castle and sheriff of Rutland, with John de Whittlebury as his deputy. One of Aldeburgh's first duties was to collect without delay an outstanding £60 which Audley owed to the king. He was permitted to retain out of that sum his wages and those of the others staying at the castle. Whittlebury had an unfortunate end, for in 1332, ten years later, he found himself imprisoned in this very castle, and in 1336 he was set upon, stabbed and beaten to death.

In spite of the political and social unrest of the times, we learn from the various inquisitions that the income which the lord of the manor derived from Oakham gradually increased. In 1237 it was worth about £60 per annum, in 1251 some £100, and by 1301 when Edmund, Earl of Cornwall, died its total value was assessed at £112.18s.11d. Even if inflation is taken into account, however, the most efficient occupiers of Oakham appear to have been Hugh de Audley and his wife Margaret. Although ousted in 1321, their dispossession was only temporary and in 1340 soon after the reversion of Oakham had been granted to William de Bohun, it was valued at £293.17s.6½d. It is from the inquisition carried out then that the extract at the beginning of this booklet is taken.

Perhaps because a very detailed survey had been taken only recently, when Hugh de Audley died in 1347 the report of the inquisition was less intimate. We do, however, gather certain glimpses of the way such a manor was run. For example, the two mills, one wind and one water, were together worth £8 annually: "but the lord of the manor provided a great deal of money for their repair when it was necessary". Or again, amongst a list of miscellaneous revenues we find that William Malkyn paid 8 shillings a year for his house and land, and no more, "because he shall flush the latrines within the castle at his own expense when necessary". At the same time, the market held every seven days on a Saturday (the Monday market is not mentioned) was worth £18 a year, and the fair held annually on the day of the Decollation of St. John the Baptist was worth 100 shillings.

It soon becomes clear that, in spite of good husbandry, the upkeep of old buildings – even the Great Hall was by now nearly 200 years old – was just as much a liability then as it is today. In the inquisition of 1361 which followed the death of Audley's successor, William de Bohun, we read these words: "There are certain buildings, namely a hall with various rooms, a chapel, a kitchen, stables, and other houses of various officers, which are worth nothing per annum (i.e. bring in no income), but with the said castle need repair and large deductions from profits each year". And again, "there is a certain watermill which is entirely ruined and worth nothing until it is rebuilt". As far as we know it never was and its site is lost: so much for the expensive repairs carried out by Audley only a few years earlier.

The succeeding years are particularly rich in recorded detail concerning Oakham Castle, for the manor remained in the king's hands from 1372 to 1386. The names of officers appointed by the crown to govern the castle, and accounts of work done, grants made, and other administrative matters, are all to be found in surviving documents. Upon the death of William de Bohun's son Humphrey, Simon de Warde was appointed steward to hold the manor in the king's name and to carry out an immediate inquisition into the state of the fief. Almost at once he was ordered to pay Nicholas de Stoke, parson of the chapel, the livery of 8 marks, 7 shillings and 1½ pence, and four loads of wood yearly, as had been the case "time out of mind". In 1373, with a local man of influence, William Flore, as surveyor, Warde and William Hakluyt, warden of the forest of Rutland, were authorised to spend up to £10 per annum on the repair of houses, walls and buildings in the manor. Flore, whose family house still stands (somewhat altered) in the High Street, was appointed receiver of all rents, farms, issues and profits of the manor and castle.

A considerable amount of work was done at the castle itself. John atte Hide, of Egleton, was controller of the works here from 1373-75, and a substantial amount of money, in all £41, was spent by John de Multon, of Manton. The great chapel and the king's two great chambers were pargeted and whitewashed, and a chimney was inserted in the chamber by the gate – perhaps the "room for the gatekeeper" mentioned in 1340. In the following year a new chapel and chamber were built, with a passageway connecting the chapel to the hall. This may not, however, have been such an extensive operation as the words imply, for the whole work, including stone walls, tiled roof and three glazed windows cost less than £30. Some of the work may have been necessary in order to prepare the castle for Edward III's last visit, in 1375, in the 49th year of his reign.

His grandson and successor, Richard II, came to Oakham in 1378 and again in 1380, when his coming necessitated further work following the appointment of surveyors to report on defects in the doors, walls, and windows. Repairs were made to the kitchen, a chimney was made for the king's chamber, and a new roasting house was built. Maintenance work on the castle buildings, some of which may possibly have been older than the hall itself, was constantly necessary. In 1382, William Sharp, tiler, was granted a writ of aid to empower him to take timber and labourers, as well as tiles and slates, for the repairs he was to carry out at Oakham and Rockingham castles, for which he was paid 4d per day. In 1385, 5000 Collyweston tiles were sent to Oakham.

The manor itself evidently continued to be a viable holding. In 1380, grants were made to William Flore of all the summer grazing in the small park of the castle, valued at 66s 8d; of £100 of the annual profits to one Richard Sturry; and of a similar amount to Thomas de Holand, Earl of Kent – the latter was an over-optimistic grant, for it transpired that the manor would produce only a further £50, and the balance had to be sought elsewhere. In 1384/5, Henry Chaundeler, the king's serjeant, was granted the office of chief bailiff of the fairs and markets of Oakham, with the attached fees and profits; but in the next year he surrendered this office, and on submitting his accounts, was awarded 10 marks per annum from the profits for life.

The officers of the castle were responsible for the smooth running of the manor and its estates, and from time to time events proved that this task was no sinecure. On one notable occasion, in 1375, there was a considerable riot between the men of Oakham, with reinforcements from Langham, on the one hand, and the inhabitants of Burley and their lord Sir Thomas le Despenser's men on the other. As a result of this riot, Burley church and churchyard were desecrated, several men were wounded by arrows or severely beaten, and peace was not restored until the constable of the castle, William de Whappelode, had been called out. We learn from the appointment of his successor, John Rukwyke, in the following year that his wages were 3d per day – a penny less than those of Sharp the tiler.

Oakham was granted to Robert de Vere, Earl of Oxford, in 1386, but he held the manor for only two years before fleeing the country in 1388. William Flore again became answerable for the manor, and once again we find that there is a surviving inquisition which gives a detailed extent in a form which by now is familiar. One aspect of its findings, however, is at first difficult to reconcile with the known record of maintenance in the immediately preceding years. This is the statement that in the castle there were simply certain buildings in a poor and ruinous state, and of no net yearly value. The Great Hall itself is not even mentioned. The implication seems to be that

*Fig. 7. The interior of the Great Hall, between 1895 and 1911, showing the former court fittings and gas flare lighting.*

most of the buildings were indeed in poor condition and suffering from general neglect and lack of maintenance, and that the work that had been done was just enough to make the castle presentable for the short period that the king stayed there. Nevertheless certain minor repairs were carried out between 1388 and 1390, when Oakham was granted to Edward, Earl of Rutland. Whatever the state of the buildings, however, the manor itself was still sufficiently profitable to produce a fair income, whether from the gardens, markets, rents, agricultural lands or woodland. It also supported the clerk or parson of the chapel, who once again had to secure possession of his office following the change of lordship.

We hear hardly anything more of the castle buildings for over a hundred years, until 1521 following the execution of the Duke of Buckingham in whose hands it then was. By then it appears to have reached its lowest ebb. In the inquisition carried out in that year, it is said that at Oakham "there is an old castle, all ruinous...; the hall is in the best state of repair, and old fashioned". It was convenient to keep it in a reasonable state and roofed solely because of the courts which were held there. Everything else was probably in a state of collapse, never to be resurrected.

It was not until George Villiers acquired the property another century later in 1621 that any serious attempt was made to put the hall itself in order. We have already seen that he erected a new pediment over the Castle Lane gateway, and it is most probable that he also re-roofed the Great Hall. Some at least of the main beams are traditionally said to have been put in by him. It may have been Villiers who levelled the ruinous buildings around the castle, and particularly the former domestic offices at the east and west ends of the hall, now that the manor was no longer required as a place in which to live, and had been superseded by the first great house at Burley-on-the-Hill.

In 1684, when James Wright illustrated the castle in his *History and Antiquities of the County of Rutland,* it was shown as standing alone within the remains of the curtain wall, in most respects in the same condition as in Buck's engraving of 1730. From the seventeenth century to the present day, the Great Hall has continued to fulfil its role as the seat of justice, with the holding of assizes, quarter sessions and petty sessions as well as coroner's inquests. We may be sure that were it not for this judicial function over the centuries, the building would have fallen into ruin and decay, for even the holding of the Great Court Leet and Court Baron of the manor ceased many years ago.

★    ★    ★

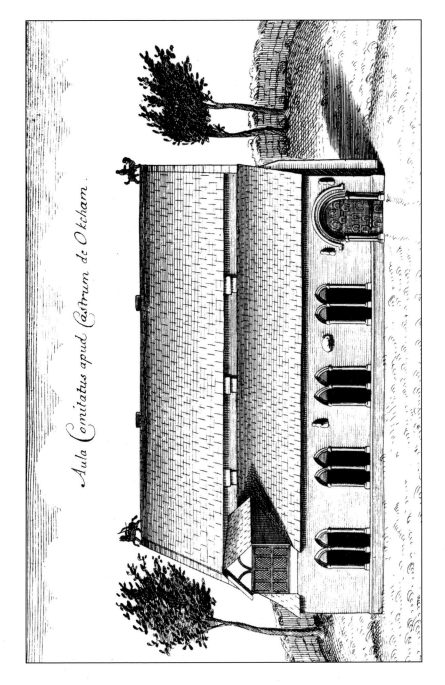

Aula Comitatus apud Castrum de Okcham.

Fig. 8.  The engraving of Oakham Castle in James Wright's History and Antiquities of the County of Rutland, 1684.

# THE LORDS OF THE MANOR

We have seen that the manor and castle of Oakham were part of the dowry of the Anglo-Saxon queens of England, and that it came finally to Edith, the wife of Edward the Confessor, in the mid-eleventh century. Edward died early in 1066, and his death was followed by the brief and harassed reign of Harold II, culminating in the upheaval of the Norman invasion led by William the Conqueror (1066-87).

The new king respected the widowed Edith's tenure of Oakham, and the manor remained in her hands until she died in 1075. Under the terms of a grant by Edward the Confessor, the whole manor should then have passed to the Abbey of Westminster. However, William I seems to have taken Oakham into his own hands, and was certainly holding it when Domesday Book was compiled in 1086. It was not until some years later that William II (1087-1100) granted to Westminster the church of Oakham and probably some, but not all, of the land. The other parts of the manor, including the site of the castle, which lies next to the church, remained in royal hands.

In this way, Oakham came to be divided into two manors, each with its own history. The church lands, governed by the Abbots and Deans of Westminster, became Oakham Deanshold. The castle and its lands, the principal manor, became Oakham Lordshold, and it is the history of this manor that we follow. A list of the lords of the manor is given on pp 38-9.

Oakham appears to have remained a royal manor until the early twelfth century, when we learn that it was held by Henry de Beaumont, who became the first Earl of Warwick. His son Roger, who succeeded him in 1119, surrendered Oakham to the king in exchange for Sutton Coldfield, and Oakham, unlike other Rutland manors, had no further connection with the Warwick overlordship.

At around this time Oakham must have come into the hands of the Ferrers family, possibly as sub-tenants of the Earls of Warwick, but we do not know exactly when this happened. Henry de Ferrers, grandson of another Henry who had been one of the Domesday commissioners, was probably holding the manor by 1130. Certainly by 1166 it was in the possession of his son Walkelin de Ferrers, a man of substance to whom the building of the Great Hall, datable on architectural grounds to soon after 1180, is correctly attributed by tradition.

Walkelin de Ferrers died in 1201 and was succeeded by his son Henry. However, when Normandy was lost to the English crown in 1205, Henry, in common with many other men who held land on both sides of the Channel, had to decide where his stronger allegiance lay. He chose to forfeit his

English lands and retired to Normandy, where the descent of his family as lords of Chambrais can be followed for 300 years until the death of the last seigneur in 1504. Henry's younger brother was already dead in 1205, but back in England his eldest sister Isabella and her husband Roger de Mortimer obtained in 1207 a grant for life of the manor and castle of Oakham, for a price of 700 marks and 7 palfreys (saddle-horses). Roger died in 1214, after which Isabella married Peter fitz Herbert, but he was dead by 1235, and she held Oakham in her own right until her own death, as an elderly widow, in 1252. The manor then reverted to the crown.

Although the Ferrers family held Oakham for a comparatively short period, perhaps only 130 years, their name and memory have lived on in association with the castle until the present day. No doubt this has much to do with the building of the Great Hall by Walkelin, but it must also owe something to the traditional surrender of horseshoes to the lord of the manor, a custom whose origins are obscure but probably lie in this period, and which is known to have been followed by Edward IV in the late fifteenth century. Although Oakham was to pass through many hands, when it was forfeited to the crown in 1521 following the execution of the Duke of Buckingham, the lands were then still described as "of the inheritance of the Lord Ferrers".

When Isabella died in 1252, the manor was valued at £100, and it was immediately granted by the king, Henry III, in part payment of a dowry of £500 promised to his younger brother Richard, Earl of Cornwall, and his heirs by his second wife Sanchia whom he had married in 1243. Richard's first wife had been Isabel, widow of Gilbert de Clare, Earl of Gloucester and Hertford, whose family is closely connected with Oakham in the next two generations.

Richard died in 1272 and he was succeeded as Earl of Cornwall by his son Edmund, cousin to Edward I. Edmund married Margaret, daughter of Richard de Clare, Earl of Gloucester, in 1272, but they were legally separated some 21 years later. He became Sheriff of Rutland in 1288 – in fact the shrievalty came to be a normal adjunct to the lordship of Oakham; and he held this office until he died without issue in 1300. The earldom became extinct, and the manor came to Edward I by inheritance. Following an inquisition, the record of which survives, the king assigned Oakham in dower to the widow Margaret, and she held it until her own death in 1312.

In 1309 Edward II granted the reversion of the manor and castle of Oakham to his much resented favourite Piers de Gaveston, whom he had created Earl of Cornwall. In fact Gaveston never held Oakham, for he was murdered shortly before Margaret, Countess of Cornwall, had died. Confusingly, however, he had himself married another Margaret de Clare, one of the three daughters of Gilbert, Earl of Gloucester, by his first wife. Gilbert married secondly Joan of Acre, the sister of Edward II, thus making Piers de Gaveston's wife the king's niece by marriage. She it was who now inherited the profits of Oakham in dower and continued to enjoy them until 1317, when she married Hugh de Audley and surrendered her dower lands to the king.

Hugh soon found surety for the price of the Oakham manor, which was granted afresh to him and his wife, and he and Margaret became joint sheriffs of Rutland. Unfortunately, however, this state of affairs did not last, for in 1321 the political trouble which had been brewing came to a head with open but unsuccessful rebellion against the king's unpopular advisers, Hugh le Despenser the elder and younger. Although Hugh the younger married Margaret's sister, Hugh de Audley had quarrelled with the Despensers; he found his lands seized, and the Audleys lost the shrievalty. The king then granted Oakham to his half-brother Edmund, Earl of Kent – not, as was the case with so much of the land seized at this time, to Hugh le Despenser. Various men then acted as constables of Oakham Castle until 1326 there was a resurgence of open revolt, the Despensers, father and son, were executed and Edward II deposed. In the first few months of his reign, Edward III ordered the Earl of Kent to surrender the castle, and returned it to Hugh and Margaret de Audley. Their original grant had been stolen in the intervening years and so Hugh had to obtain a copy of his letters patent. He and his wife were restored to the shrievalty of Rutland, and in 1336 he was created Earl of Gloucester, a title which had become extinct upon the death of his brother-in-law Gilbert at Bannockburn in 1314, and was to do so again when he himself died five years after Margaret in 1347. Of the principal characters in this troubled episode, few attained such a peaceful end.

Hugh and Margaret de Audley had died without issue, and although Margaret had a daughter by Piers de Gaveston, she could not succeed to her mother's estates. The future of the castle had, however, already been assured in 1337, when Edward III had granted the reversion of Oakham to William de Bohun, lately created Earl of Northampton, together with other lands to the value of £1000 to support his new estate as an earl. Until he could enter into possession in 1347, the loss of income was made up in payments from shipping dues.

William de Bohun was succeeded in 1361 by his son Humphrey, who did not come of age until two years later. Humphrey died young, in 1372, but he had married and left a widow, Joan, and two daughters; of Joan and their daughter Eleanor we hear more later. At the time, however, Oakham, unlike most of Humphrey's lands, reverted to the crown because it could pass to male heirs only, and Joan had only a temporary grant of Langham, which was part of the manor.

Oakham remained in the king's hands for fourteen years, from 1372 to 1386. The manor was then granted by the young Richard II to his friend and cousin Robert de Vere, Earl of Oxford. His tenure, however, was short-lived, for in the political turmoil of the next two years he was convicted of treason, forfeited his estates and fled the country. In 1390 Oakham was granted to Edward, Earl of Rutland, the eldest son of Edmund de Langley, Duke of York, to whom the reversion had been promised in 1386. The reversion now was granted to his uncle, Thomas de Woodstock, Duke of Gloucester, who had married Eleanor, the daughter of Humphrey and Joan de Bohun.

Thomas de Woodstock, however, was spitefully murdered in 1397, at the instigation of Richard II. His only son and heir, Humphrey, could not succeed to his father's honours because of his attainder, and died unmarried in 1399, the year in which Richard II met his own violent end. In 1401, Henry IV confirmed Edward, Earl of Rutland, in possession, provided that he rendered yearly a rose at midsummer. Edward died without issue at the battle of Agincourt in 1415, but by then he had lost possession of Oakham.

In 1414, the manor was claimed for the third time, and successfully, by Sir William Bourchier, the second husband of Anne, the daughter and heiress of Thomas de Woodstock and Eleanor de Bohun. It was held that Oakham had been wrongly granted to the Earl of Rutland in 1390, and that the proper descent was to Anne in right of her mother, Eleanor de Bohun, daughter of Humphrey de Bohun who had died in 1372. This judgement must have brought satisfaction to one other person who had watched all the sad troubles of these turbulent years – namely, Humphrey's widow for 47 years, Joan de Bohun, who lived until 1419.

Sir William Bourchier and his wife held Oakham until his death in 1438, when the manor and castle passed to Humphrey, Earl of Stafford, her son by her first husband Edmund, Earl of Stafford. Humphrey was created Duke of Buckingham in 1444, and met his death at the battle of Northampton in 1459. His widow, Anne de Neville, held Oakham in dower until she died in 1480. Their son Humphrey, a staunch Lancastrian like his father, had been killed at the first battle of St Albans in 1455, and it was Humphrey's posthumous son Henry Stafford who succeeded to the honours and estates of the Duke of Buckingham. Henry was of great service in securing the accession of Richard III in 1483, but he quickly became disillusioned with the new king, and joined in the plot to place another protégé, the Earl of Richmond, on the throne. For his part in this, he was beheaded without legal trial in November of that year. His lands were forfeited to the crown, and Oakham was granted to Henry de Grey, Lord of Codnor.

Richard III, however, reigned for less than three years. In 1485, the victorious Henry VII made void the attainder of 1483, by which the Buckingham lands had been forfeited, dispossessed Grey, and restored Oakham to Henry Stafford's eight-year-old son and heir Edward, Duke of Buckingham. Edward eventually obtained the livery of his estates from the king in 1508, but fell foul of Cardinal Wolsey, was found guilty of high treason, and was executed in 1521 by Henry VIII. The manor now reverted to the king, who appointed a chief steward in 1522. The death of Buckingham's widow, Eleanor, in 1530, ended this unfortunate family's association with Oakham. No less than five generations, from Thomas de Woodstock to Edward Stafford, had met their deaths either on the scaffold or on the battlefield.

In less than 280 years, from 1252 to 1530, there had been some 24 changes of lordship or grants of reversion. Nonetheless, virtually all those who had held Oakham through this period were closely related by descent or by marriage not only with each other but with the Angevin kings of England. From now onwards the situation changes.

Henry VIII held Oakham until 1536, when he granted the manor to Thomas Cromwell, whom he had created Baron Cromwell earlier in the year. But, in the words of Dugdale, "as his rise was somewhat hasty, so was his fall very sudden", and he was beheaded in 1540, only three months after having been created Earl of Essex. He was succeeded at Oakham in turn by his eldest son Gregory and grandson Henry, for Oakham had been settled on them in 1538, before his disgrace. The manor then came in 1592 to Edward, 4th Lord Cromwell, who obtained licence in 1596 to sell it to Sir John Harington. The property had never before been sold, for it had always remained in the overlordship of the crown, and it was now for the first time possessed outright by someone other than the sovereign.

Sir John was created Baron Harington of Exton by James I at his coronation in 1603, became tutor to the king's daughter Princess Elizabeth, and died of a fever at Worms in 1613. His second and only surviving son John died of smallpox in 1614, whereupon the barony became extinct; Oakham remained in the hands of Sir John's widow, Anne, Lady Harrington, until her death in 1620. It passed then to their daughter, Lucy, wife of Edward, Earl of Bedford, who in turn sold the manor in 1621 to George Villiers, who was created

Duke of Buckingham in 1623. Buckingham cut a splendid figure and, in spite of his youth, had extraordinary influence first over James I and then over Charles I, and was correspondingly unpopular. He was stabbed to death at Portsmouth in 1628, at the age of 36.

Buckingham had married Lady Catherine Manners, the heiress of Francis, Earl of Rutland, and Oakham was now inherited by their nine-month-old son George. During the Commonwealth, the Buckingham estates were assigned to Sir Thomas Fairfax, the parliamentary general. With great foresight, the second Duke of Buckingham married Fairfax's daughter Mary in 1657, and with her was able to regain a considerable portion of his estates even before the Restoration. Such was his profligate extravagance, however, that he was obliged to sell his estates shortly before he died in 1687, and the manor and castle of Oakham were bought by Daniel Finch, 2nd Earl of Nottingham, who in 1694-1708 built a new mansion at Burley-on-the-Hill on the site of the manorial seat, which had been burnt by Parliamentary forces in 1646. He succeeded to the earldom of Winchelsea only a year before his death in 1730 at the age of 82, having fathered at least 25 children by his two wives.

Nottingham was succeeded by his fourth but first surviving son Daniel, Earl of Winchelsea and Nottingham, MP for Rutland from 1710-30, who died in 1769. His nephew George, 9th Earl of Winchelsea, served as Lord Lieutenant of Rutland from 1779 until his death in 1826. The titles then went to a cousin, but Oakham, with Burley and other Rutland estates, were inherited by his adopted son George Finch. He died in 1870, and was succeeded by his son the Rt. Hon. G. H. Finch, MP for Rutland for 40 years, until he died in 1907. It was in G. H. Finch's memory that the Great Hall was restored in a programme of work completed in 1911, and a marble bust of him by F. W. Pomeroy was unveiled in 1913. He was followed by his sons A. G. Finch (d.1914) and W. H. Finch (d.1939). When the latter died, the estates passed to a great-nephew, Major J. R. Hanbury.

In 1944, the Castle and its grounds were given by Major Hanbury to the Rutland County Council. Upon local government reorganisation in 1974, it passed to the Leicestershire County Council, being cared for by the Museums Service for the county. In 1997, this situation was reversed and Oakham Castle came back into the hands of the reconstituted Rutland County Council. And so the lord of the manor, now Mr. E. R. Hanbury, no long has the custody of the castle, where the history of his inheritance began so long ago.

★　　　★　　　★

# TWELFTH CENTURY SCULPTURE
## AT OAKHAM CASTLE

✱   ✱   ✱

*by*
### *Robin Emmerson*

The Great Hall of Oakham Castle was built for Walkelin de Ferrers, who was in possession of Oakham by 1166 and died in 1201. The hall, however, can be dated more closely to between 1180 and 1190. It is the earliest aisled hall of stone in Britain to have survived more or less complete. It is also the earliest secular building in Britain in which we can still appreciate a scheme of figure-sculpture. The carvings are made of the fine-grained, golden oolitic limestone quarried not far away at Clipsham in Rutland.

## THE INTERIOR

It has long been known where the sculptors came from. This is because the capitals of the arcades at Oakham (fig. 10) are of an unusual form, which was introduced into this country at the choir of Canterbury Cathedral, begun in 1175 (fig. 11). The chronicle of the monk Gervase gives us detailed knowledge of the progress of work on the Canterbury choir. It was built in its present form by a French master-mason, William of Sens. In the autumn of 1178 he was crippled by a fall from some scaffolding, and work on the eastern parts of the cathedral beyond the choir was taken over and continued by another William, known as the Englishman. He completed the east end of the cathedral in 1184. The capitals of the choir arcades at Canterbury are certainly the work of French sculptors, because their foliage decoration is just like that in a group of churches to the north-east of Paris.

It is recorded that William of Sens distributed templates for shaping the stones to the sculptors at Canterbury. With aids of this sort, English craftsmen could copy the structure of the arcade capitals but not the complicated French type of foliage. The lesser capitals which they carved for the aisles and upper parts of the cathedral building are therefore decorated with simpler, flat leaves (fig. 12).

The combination of flat leaves with the basic structure of the choir arcade capitals is just what we find in the Oakham arcade capitals (fig. 10). The abacus, or slab above each capital, even has its corners cut off just as at

9. *The musician at Oakham Castle to which the single
surviving head may belong.*

Canterbury. This strongly suggests, therefore, that the carvers of the Oakham capitals were Englishmen who had worked at Canterbury between 1175 and 1184.

In one place at Oakham an attempt was made to produce more complicated and lifelike leaves: this is on the corner of capital 1 (see plan, fig. 24) facing the west wall and what is now the judge's bench. The reason was no doubt that the lord sat there, at the end opposite the doors to the kitchens, and this capital would be in his line of view.

*10. Arcade capital at Oakham Castle.*

*11. Choir arcade capital at*
*Canterbury Cathedral*

Above each capital, on the inner side facing the body of the hall, is the figure of a musician. All six figures have had their heads knocked off at some time. Four of them are human: two of the instruments which they are playing can certainly be identified, a fiddle (above capital 1, and fig. 13) and a psaltery (2 and fig. 15 – it is similar to a zither). The other two figures are of animals – an ass with a rote (3 – similar to a harp) and a goat playing a rebec with a bow (6, and fig. 14). Animal musicians were a favourite subject of the Kentish school of sculpture, centred on Canterbury. The most famous example is found on a capital in the crypt of the cathedral, dating from the beginning of the twelfth century: it shows an ass with a harp, a ram with a rebec, and a goat and a dog with recorders. The outlines of the human musicians at Oakham (fig. 9) also resemble earlier work of the Kent sculptors, for example some apostles on the lintel of the west door at Rochester Cathedral.

In the collections of the Rutland County Museum in Oakham there is a stone head, discovered while the foundations for the post office were being excavated, on the site of the castle moat, near the entrance by Castle Lane. The stone appears to be of the same type as the rest of the sculpture. Figure 9 shows it in place on the musician (no. 4) to which it may well have belonged. All the figures of the musicians have a projecting rib at the back of the neck, just as the head does, but this figure is the best fit. The head is large in proportion to the body, but this is quite common in sculpture of the period.

12. *Triforium capitals at Canterbury Cathedral.*

13. *Musician playing a fiddle.*

14. *Goat playing a rebec.*

15. *Musician playing a psaltery.*

Above each capital, on the side facing into the aisle, is a head beautifully carved in the round. They are the corbels which once supported the aisle roofs. The heads above capitals 2 and 3 both appear to be wearing a muzzle or "scold's bridle". At either end of the hall, the arcade arches come to rest on large ornate corbels, each of which is carved as a lion on top of two human heads (fig. 16). These heads especially have a naturalism which is a new and exciting element in late twelfth century art, and which contrasts strangely with the stylised drapery of the musician figures.

During restoration work in the cloisters of Canterbury Cathedral, many fragments of sculpture were found. They had been re-used as building material, but probably many of them originally form part of a choir-screen which is known to have been erected in 1180. Some of the figures (fig. 17) have a wonderfully naturalistic treatment of the heads and drapery. The modelling of some of the faces at Oakham suggests that their sculptors had

16. *One of the Oakham corbels.*

17. *Sculpture fragment from Canterbury Cathedral.*

seen work of this kind. In other respects the work at Oakham is more traditional: the hair was still treated a series of braided locks (fig. 18), and the sculptor of the musicians represented the drapery by a pattern of lines in the way with which he was familiar.

Where the arcades meet the walls at either end of the hall there are small label-stops carved as the heads of animals and birds, above each corbel to the left and right (fig. 19). The three-dimensional treatment of the eye-sockets connects them with works of the Kentish school.

18. *A corbel head.*        19. *Owl label-stop.*

# THE EXTERIOR

Buck's view of 1730 (fig. 5) shows five figures attached to the south wall, with space for at least one other. The two which he shows immediately to the left of the doorway have disappeared: the others are the three still in place. The two figures now missing had already disappeared when J. Clayton drew the building in 1847. His drawing shows that by then the doorway had been moved to its present position. It is strange that he does not show the figure which is furthest on the left in Buck's view, and is still there today. Instead, Clayton shows a figure at the far left end of the wall: restorers probably put it there to match the one still in place at the far right end. Inside the hall is the figure, now loose, of a lion-like animal sitting up on its hindquarters, which may have formed part of this external sculpture. The figure to the left of the present doorway represents a man astride a beast, grasping its neck in one hand and its tail in the other. The windows in the south wall have in their jambs capitals with flat overlapping leaves like some of the minor capitals in the choir at Canterbury. The window at the right-hand end has sprays of foliage in the two heads, and it appears from Buck's view that the window at the left end once did also.

On top of the gable at either end of the hall stands a carved finial: at one end is Samson and the lion, at the other a centaur (fig. 20) whose bow is broken away. Gable figures seldom survive, for they are vulnerable, but others of the twelfth century exist not far away, on the transept and porch of Southwell Minster in Nottinghamshire. At the monastery of St. Maurice d'Agaune in Switzerland there survives a late twelfth century silver ciborium of English workmanship (fig. 21): the bowl is embellished with figures which resemble the Canterbury fragments mentioned earlier. The lid is crowned by the figure of another centaur, Chiron, instructing the young Achilles. Since the arts were at that time rated in importance according to the cost of their materials, it was quite common for sculptors to derive designs from work in precious metals.

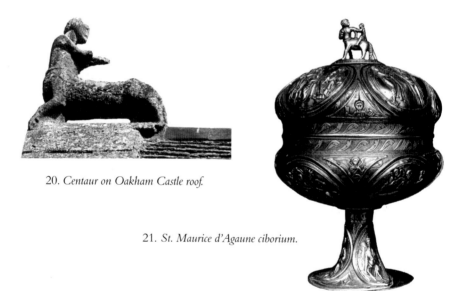

*20. Centaur on Oakham Castle roof.*

*21. St. Maurice d'Agaune ciborium.*

## DATING

The sculptors who worked at Oakham left their mark on at least two other buildings in the vicinity. Of the large twelfth century church at Grantham, Lincolnshire, several nave piers survive with their capitals, and at Twyford in Leicestershire the nave of the little church has three capitals (fig. 22). The style of these carvings is so similar to Oakham that they must all have been made by the same sculptors. It may have been the prospect of work at Oakham or at some other building now demolished that brought them from Canterbury to the Midlands. It should also be noted that at this time Twyford was part of the manorial holding of Oakham.

22. *Capital at Twyford Church.*

23. *Crouching figure below
the east window (interior).*

We cannot be sure at what stage these men left the works at Canterbury. The capitals from the cathedral illustrated here (figs. 11 and 12) were carved not later than 1178. The sculptors may have left at any time after then. Many of the capitals set up by William the Englishman after that date have new features which are not found at Oakham. However, it is likely that the sculptors left Canterbury only when there was no longer work for them. In 1183 no work was done because funds had temporarily run out. After the completion of the cathedral in 1184, all the craftsmen must have sought work elsewhere. The sculptures at Oakham were therefore probably carved between 1180 and 1190.

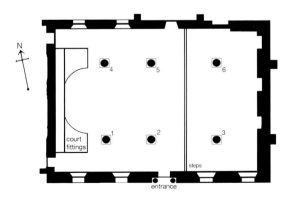

24. *Plan of Oakham Castle: the column numbers relate to the text.*

## Holders of Oakham Castle and Lords of the Manor of Oakham

AD   964   Aelfthrith, wife of Edgar
1002   Emma, wife of Aethelred II and Cnut
1052   Edith, wife of Edward the Confessor
1075   William I
11 ??   Henry de Beaumont (Newburgh), Earl of Warwick
1119   Roger, Earl of Warwick
1119   Henry I
? 1130   Henry de Ferrers
by 1166   Walkelin de Ferrers
1201   Henry de Ferrers
1205   John
1207   Isabella de Ferrers and Roger de Mortimer (d.1214)
1252   Richard, Earl of Cornwall
1272   Edmund, Earl of Cornwall (m. Margaret de Clare I)
1300   Edward I: Margaret de Clare I in dower
1309   Reversion to Piers de Gaveston (m. Margaret de Clare II: d.1312)
1312   Margaret de Clare II in dower
1317   Margaret de Clare II and Hugh de Audley
1321   Edmund, Earl of Kent
1326   Hugh and Margaret de Audley restored (cr. Earl of Gloucester)
1337   Reversion to William de Bohun, Earl of Northampton
1347   William de Bohun, Earl of Northampton
1361   Humphrey de Bohn, Earl of Northampton
1372   Edward III
1377   Richard II
1386   Robert de Vere, Earl of Oxford; reversion to Edmund de Langley, Duke of York
1388   Richard II
1390   Edward, Earl of Rutland, son of Edmund de Langley; reversion to Thomas de Woodstock, Duke of Gloucester (d.1397)
1414   Sir William Bourchier and Anne de Woodstock
1438   Humphrey, Earl of Stafford, later Duke of Buckingham
1459   Anne de Neville, in dower
1480   Henry, Duke of Buckingham
1483   Henry Grey, Lord of Codnor
1485   Edward, Duke of Buckingham
1521   Eleanor, Duchess of Buckingham, in dower
1530   Henry VIII
1536   Thomas, Lord Cromwell
1540   Gregory, Lord Cromwell

| 1551 | Henry, Lord Cromwell |
|------|----------------------|
| 1592 | Edward, Lord Cromwell |
| 1596 | Sir John Harington, later Baron Harington |
| 1613 | John, Lord Harington |
| 1614 | Anne, Lady Harington |
| 1620 | Lucy, Countess of Bedford |
| 1621 | George Villiers, later Duke of Buckingham |
| 1628 | George, Duke of Buckingham (m. Mary Fairfax) |
| 1651 | Sir Thomas Fairfax |
| 1657 | George, Duke of Buckingham (restored) |
| 1687 | Daniel, Earl of Winchelsea and Nottingham |
| 1769 | George, Earl of Winchelsea and Nottingham |
| 1826 | George Finch |
| 1870 | Rt. Hon. George Henry Finch MP |
| 1907 | Alan George Finch |
| 1914 | Wilfred Henry Finch |
| 1939 | Major James Robert Hanbury |
| 1944 | Gift of the Castle to Rutland County Council |
| 1971 | Evan Robert Hanbury |

## Further Reading

The most important single printed source remains *Victoria County History, Rutland* I (1908), II (1935), which contains detailed manorial history supported by references to original documents. Abstracts of many of these are to be found in the various Calendars published by the Public Record Office. Oakham manor court rolls dating from 1694 to 1935 (but incomplete) are deposited in the Record Office for Leicestershire, Leicester & Rutland, Long Street, Wigston Magna, Leicester, LE18 2AH.

Biographical details of many of the lords of the manor are given in the volumes of G. E. Cokayne's *Complete Peerage*, and an account of the horseshoes which they received appears in T. H. McK. Clough, *The Horseshoes of Oakham Castle* (3rd ed., 1999).

The only local antiquarian account of Oakham is in James Wright, *History and Antiquities of the County of Rutland* (1684), and the first detailed description of the castle is by the Rev. C. H. Hartshorne, "The Hall of Oakham", *Archaeological Journal* V (1848) 124 – 42 (later reprinted in *Leicestershire & Rutland Notes & Queries II*).

There are two general accounts of the castle: Pearl Finch, *Oakham Castle* (1903), and by A. Hamilton Thompson in *The Story of Oakham Church, School and Castle* (n.d. but about 1930). The archaeological finds from the Post Office site are published by P. Gathercole, "Excavations at Oakham Castle", *Transactions of the Leicestershire Archaeol. & Hist. Soc.* XXXIV (1958) 17– 38.

For the sculptural context see G. Zarnecki, *Later English Romanesque Sculpture 1140– 1210* (Tiranti, 1953).

For the link with Canterbury see J. P. Cave, "The Canterbury Choir Capitals", in *The Friends of Canterbury Cathedral Annual Report* (1936), 59. The contemporary account by the monk Gervase of the rebuilding of Canterbury Cathedral is translated in Robert Willis, *The Architectural History of Canterbury Cathedral* (London, 1845; reprint Paul B. Minet, Chicheley, 1972). Two unpublished works are also important: Malcolm Thurlby, *Transitional Sculpture in England* (Ph.D. thesis, University of East Anglia, 1976) and Rosalyn Mair, *The Canterbury Choir Capitals* (M. A. report, Courtauld Institute of Art, 1977).

For the general artistic context in which Oakham Castle was built and decorated, see Sarah Macready and F. H. Thompson (eds.), *Art and Patronage in the English Romanesque* (Society of Antiquaries, London 1986) and for a local architectural context see N. Pevsner, *The Buildings of England: Leicestershire and Rutland* (2nd ed., Penguin, 1984).

## Acknowledgements

The authors wish to thank the following for their assistance in preparing the original edition of this booklet and their comments both on the castle and on the text: Mr. J. L. Barber, Mr. G. A. Chinnery, Mrs. J. I. Clough, Mrs. E. M.Martyn, Mr. C. E. Owen, Dr. A. J. Taylor, Dr. M. Thurlby and Professor G. Zarnecki. The illustrations are reproduced from historic negatives, photographs and originals in the possession of the Rutland County Museum, except for copyright photographs in the chapter on the sculptures which are reproduced with the permision of the Courtauld Institute, London (figs. 3, 4 and 9) and the Marburg Institut (fig. 14).

Front Cover Photograph: Mr R.J.A. Adams

Published by Rutland County Council
Catmose Street, Oakham, Rutland, LE15 6HP

Third Edition
Copyright © Rutland County Council District Council 1999

First published by Leicestershire Museums, Arts & Records Service for the Friends of the Rutland County Museum 1981
Second edition with corrections 1987

Distributed by Rutland County Museum,
Catmose Street, Oakham, Rutland, LE15 6HW

Printed by deVoyle Litho, Rural Industries, John O'Gaunt, Leicestershire

ISBN 0 9536627 0 5